A Home For Turtle

Written by Kerrie Shanahan

Illustrated by Chantal Stewart

Flying Start
to Literacy®

One day I saw a turtle in the park.

"Can I have this turtle for a pet?" I said.

"No," said Dad.

"We do not have a pond.
A turtle must have water
to swim in."

"Let's go to the pond," I said.

So Dad and I
went to the pond.

I let the turtle go.

The turtle jumped
into the pond.

It swam in the water.

Then the turtle
sat on a log in the sun.

"Snap!"

The turtle got an insect
to eat.

"A pond is the best spot
for this turtle," I said.